# Imagine
# Being More
# Afraid
# of Freedom
# than
# Slavery

# Imagine Being More Afraid of Freedom than Slavery

POEMS

## Pamela Sneed

AN IMPRINT OF FORDHAM UNIVERSITY PRESS

NEW YORK   2023

Fordham University Press has no responsibility for the persistence or accuracy of URLs for external or third-party Internet websites referred to in this publication and does not guarantee that any content on such websites is, or will remain, accurate or appropriate.

Fordham University Press also publishes its books in a variety of electronic formats. Some content that appears in print may not be available in electronic books.

Visit us online at www.fordhampress.com/new-york-relit/.

Library of Congress Cataloging-in-Publication Data available online at https://catalog.loc.gov.

Designed by Michelle McMillian

Printed in the United States of America
25 24 23   5 4 3 2 1

*In Memory of Don Reid*

*There was a time when you were not a slave,*
*remember that.*
*Make an effort to remember,*
*or failing that,*
*invent.*

—Monique Wittig

# Contents

Acknowledgments      xi

Preface: Genesis      xiii

## Part One

Languages I've Never Learned      5

The Final Solution      6

The Silver Badge      8

Eyes on the Prize      13

Incest      15

Jealousy      16

Precious Crazy Girl Giggles      17

Why Did You Have to Be a Poet?      18

*I haven't told you*      20

Blues Suite      21

Elegy      22

Rapunzel      23

Underestimation of Power      24

Teaching      26

Stretch Marks and Cellulite      28

New York      31

| | |
|---|---|
| *When we broke up* | 32 |
| Planet of the Apes | 33 |
| It Is Not a New Age | 35 |

## Part Two

| | |
|---|---|
| The Woods | 39 |
| *History hasn't told the truth about* | |
| *revolutionaries* | 41 |
| Monologue to God | 42 |
| *Dear God,* | 44 |
| The Artist | 46 |
| The Revolutionary | 48 |
| Helpful Hints for an Aspiring Martyr | 52 |
| Woman in Love 1 | 53 |
| Woman in Love 2 | 55 |
| Imagine Being More Afraid of Freedom | |
| than Slavery | 57 |
| Epilogue: Runaway | 63 |

# Acknowledgments

Special thanks to Tracy Sherrod, Marie Brown, Eve Sandler, Christian Haye, Mimi Gonzalez, Alisa Lebow, Cynthia Madansky, Milagros Diaz, Carla Jackson Brewer, and Darryl Turner.

Thanks to Carol Ramer, Wanda Acosta, Tony Clark, John Jusino, Paul Beatty, The Boston Writers Room, Jack Tilton Gallery, Hilton Als, Dorothy Randall-Grey, Cheryl Sneed, and Sophie Morrocock.

Grateful acknowledgment is made to the following publications, where these poems first appeared, in different versions: "Languages I've Never Learned," "Jealousy," and "Precious Crazy Girl Giggles" first appeared in *The Arc of Love*, 1996. "Languages I've Never Learned" also appeared in *Tribes* magazine, 1994. "The Final Solution" appeared in *Aloud: Voices from the Nuyorican Poets Cafe*, 1994. An excerpt of "The Revolutionary" first appeared in *The Portable Lower East Side*, 1994. "The Revolutionary" and "Helpful Hints for an Aspiring Martyr" appeared in *Changing America*, 1995. "Why Did You Have to Be a Poet?" appeared in *Ikon*, 1994. "Rapunzel" appeared in *Tribute to Mumia Jamal*, 1996. "Imagine Being More Afraid of Freedom than Slavery" and "The Woods" first appeared in *The New Fuck You*, 1995.

# Preface: Genesis

I was apprehensive at first to read the whole of *Imagine Being More Afraid of Freedom than Slavery* from start to finish. Of course over the years I've read segments and assigned it as a reading to students. Through them and myself I've witnessed and felt the text's great emotional impact and timeliness. Still I wasn't sure how it would feel as a whole 25 years after its first publication. In many regards, I've grown and am a different person. Though a few pages in I clearly saw the continuum between then and now, That raw and honest voice, that thirst and demand for justice, entwinement of the personal, political, historical and that sometimes flash of humor are all still present. Reading I was able to see the courage of me and admire it. I also admire as a poet, an interdisciplinary artist, an activist, a Professor, I've fulfilled my life's purpose & intent stated in these pages of walking in the footsteps of my favorite revolutionaries and truth tellers Audre Lorde, Assata Shakur and Harriet Tubman. As Tina Turner once said of her career, "I've stayed the course."

I often speak of my early years growing up in church. My grandfather was a Baptist minister, and his wife, my grandmother Pearl, was the First Lady. It was from that language and song and testimonies of Black people, the preachers, their wives, and the parishioners I first learned poetry, and theater too. Using the analogy then of the church and the Bible, *Imagine Being More Afraid of Freedom than Slavery* is clearly not only my first book; it is my genesis. And it marks my coming into formation as a young Black lesbian poet.

Reading these pages I can see and imagine clearly the black clunky shoes I wore (probably men's) as I stole away from Boston and its suburbs to become myself. I will never forget landing first in the South Bronx (but that's a whole other story) and the day a friend helped me shave my head. I can see the mid- to late '80s and the black leggings and white men's tank tops I wore attending The New School. I won't forget the second-floor classrooms in the 11th Street building, where I was educated and looked out onto the trees through large glass windows. I can still see the tables and desks where I first learned about, read, and discussed Toni Morrison. There, I was also reared on South Africa's anti-apartheid struggle. Nelson and Winnie Mandela were parents to a whole generation of activists worldwide. I can recall almost the exact day when I gave birth to myself. I was in a professor's office, surrounded by books. I turned in a paper late about Black feminism/admiring Black women who weren't in the course curriculum. Ann Snitow, a famous feminist writer, was in residence at The New School then. She attended that meeting with my professor and me, and after I read, she semi-danced around the office and said, describing me in the most melodious voice, "She's a writer! She's a writer!" On that day I became fully Pamela Sneed, the poet.

In the pages of *Imagine* I also remember my first poetry teacher, the late, great Sekou Sundiata. He taught me the poetic forms. I remember his brown velvet skin, smooth voice. I was one of the students who fought to integrate The New School/Lang College, to bring its first Black professors. Sekou was a result of that fight. I also came of age in the bars and clubs of the East Village and its poetry and performance scene. I also discovered The Center center on 13th Street where Black and Brown LGBTQIA poetry readings were held. At the Center, I eventually met and read and held court with some of the fiercest women of color poets of the time.

After college, my first job was running an after-school center for LGBTQIA youth at The Hetrick Martin Institute. At its former location on the West Side Highway, across from the piers, I encountered the young and adult LGBTQIA people who would inform the basis of my work and ongoing commitment to social justice. It was through the stories, the heartbreaks, struggles and triumphs of queer people I shaped myself. Hetrick Martin was my first home. Many of the poems in this book were written and conceived just as the devastation of AIDS was beginning to take hold. My close friend at the time, poet Donald Woods, had heard the titular poem from this collection but didn't live to see the second half of this book realized as a stage play. It premiered at the Nuyorican Poets Café. I recall that after the playI spoke to the now-deceased poet Colin Robinson. He was speaking of watching me perform and said, "I saw Donald there." I had also felt Donald's presence in the room, like an angel watching over me.

What I haven't yet said is that *Imagine* was written after my first big heartbreak. I had fallen in love with another poet I'd met performing at Hunter College in a piece called "Stations." I believed she was the woman of my dreams and was devastated that it didn't work out. I didn't believe anyone could experience the depth of sorrow I felt after our breakup. I wrote *Imagine* to survive it. At that time, I also remember a quote by Toni Morrison that said, in effect, "Write the stories you want or need to read." I also didn't want another woman to go to the library and not have the words.

As I re-read *Imagine*, apprehension turned to curiosity as to how the poems would affect me now. "Helpful Hints for an Aspiring Martyr" made me laugh out loud. Other poems still made me wince with pain. Even though I've overcome and worked through so much fear, self-hatred, and trauma, the title poem still rings with vitality and challenge: *Imagine Being More Afraid of Freedom than Slavery*. I am proud to say that fear no longer immobilizes me. However, as I told my writing students recently, like fear, breaking silence is not a one-time event. It's an ongoing process, much like freedom. Breaking one chain can give you strength to break another.

The poems and perspectives in this collection are clear-eyed. It's easier to discern where characters like the Revolutionary are meant to be read satirically. For years, there were people who thought, based on that character, that I didn't believe in therapy. Nothing could be further from the truth. I'm a lifelong therapy person. And the poem "Incest," which once read as startling, is more neutral. It was meant to be read as figurative, not literal, and I hate what the confusion did.

People still write to me and tell me *Imagine* changed their lives, gave them the courage to leave an abusive relationship, or to be true to themselves. What I'm hoping to describe here is the journey of how a Black girl from the suburbs and a working-class background, reared for factory work, abandoned thrice over, adopted, physically and mentally abused, never meant to survive, as Audre Lorde declared, but who found purpose and the will to live through poetry.

Even though the AIDS crisis, misogyny, racism and racist violence, and crimes against LGBTQIA people are still prevalent and have destroyed so much, the world feels much more dangerous to me now. I am frightened by the overturning of *Roe v. Wade*, anti-trans legislation, the mass shootings, COVID-19, the rise again of white supremacy. In some twisted irony, Black bodies have less value in the present day than they did in slavery. As I wrote once about Mike Brown, allegedly murdered over a stolen cigar box, at least in slavery he might still be alive. The punishment for stealing might be a toe, finger, or foot cut off. Now it's shoot to kill. Thinking of this, I contemplate the lines from *Imagine* which could hold the answer and antidote: "If we owned ourselves we could overturn this Earth"—meaning if we were able to harness our own power, we could cultivate and achieve positive change in this world. This is the ultimate lesson I've learned and am imparting from my life in and from the church of poetry.

Pamela Sneed
2023

Imagine
Being More
Afraid
of Freedom
than
Slavery

# Part One

# Languages I've Never Learned

She collected women like trophies
assorted shapes, sizes,
colors, contours
Each affirmed her ability
to make even modest women
want to climb inside her skin
like soldiers seeking refuge
from the storm.

She never stayed long enough to love
only enough to ignite their attention
but when they began to clear their closets
she talked of traveling
and needing a larger space.

I knew I never should have
gotten involved with that woman
I knew I never should have
gotten involved with that woman
part of her power being
she was a bad butch
who made women unravel
come undone at the seams
like Wonder Woman beneath her armor
was desperate.

I knew I never should have
gotten involved with that woman
But, somewhere inside she moved me
to another country
and I started speaking in
languages I've never learned.

# The Final Solution

Last night in your arms
touching your tongue to mine
I forgot
lesbianism is an illness
caused by a deficiency of good dick
which might mean this love
lingering on my lips is a disease
according to our parents
in their individual states
who chant daily with
the moral majority on channel 5
for our exile from society

In your arms I couldn't see
the man behind us screaming
I was unnatural
his behavior was unnatural
so I crossed the street
afraid he'd give me some good dick
and I'd be found in an alley
with my vagina ripped open
and my panties stuffed
in my mouth

This morning as I dreamt
of you last night
a well-known newspaper
in the Black community
printed a letter saying
we should be made to wear

stars on our clothes
be forced into ghetto camps
and if our perversion
is still not cured
there will be a final solution.

# The Silver Badge

1.
Kim had Black velvet skin.
She was 5 foot 1
with shoulder-length Black hair
bird-like features
and remnants of baby fat.
Her family moved
from Chicago to Boston's suburb
presumably for a better life
oxygen and green grass
to escape shackling poverty
gang wars
and the notorious crimes
of Chicago's Southside.

My cousin Lisa and I were a gang
of suburb Black girls
unified by isolation that made us sisters
when we weren't.
After school we'd peruse Boston's inner city
look for boys
new styles to imitate.
On Saturday nights and weekends
we snuck into 18 and over dance clubs.
At 14, I was fearful of Kim's city ways
how she cussed and swore,
and displayed what we most wanted
a kick-ass spirit
open and long-legged defiance.

We were trained for docility, factory work
to divorce city Blacks
settle quietly

peacefully integrate
lead crisp cotton, pleated pant
Sunday school existence.

For us Black was George Jefferson on tv
and history that made white kids turn to look at us
It was King Kong, Muhammad Ali and someone
who knew nothing about birthing babies.

It was Martin and Coretta King
Black limousines
Black veils
sometimes being proud
of having trees and green grass
and never having to touch the city's concrete.

Both Kim and her Mom were singers
with guts like Aretha and Etta
voices that knew hunger
and the strain of lost love.
Kim surpassed
the blue bobby sock uniformity
of high school glee club.
After school I sat in her wallpapered kitchen
as she sang over and over
Chaka Khan's "In Love We Grow"
*we go on and on*
*from dawn to dawn*

She was lonely to have left
all she knew
never spoke of fathers or
the Southside streets.

There was a war between her and her Mom
that had to do with Kim's attitude

I'd hear them argue
behind bedroom doors
and Kim emerging to say
I can't stand my mother.
I think it must have been
they were mirrors of each other
the same person years apart.
Sometimes on Saturday or Sunday
Kim's Mom entertained
opened a bottle of liqueur
and let us all taste
then she and Kim would join voices
singing in Baptist unison
and it's the only time I remember
them both happy.

2.
One day, my cousin Lisa, Kim and I
snuck into Kim's Mom's bedroom
with the zebra rug
red lava lamp
and Black lacquer dresser.
We had just smoked a joint
sat circular on the carpet
when Kim stood up
as she sometimes did
with bottle in hand
and said "I'm gonna be a hoe
make money
and fuck anyone I want."
We laughed, doubted her.
Months later, Kim's first boyfriend
was a notorious pimp
denounced as a suburb Black.
He lacked the clean-cut style

his skin scarred and yellow.
Afterwards, Kim started to skip school
and disappeared from our circle.

3.
Saturday night
I had gone to buy stockings
and passed Kim's house en route
to the department store.
Through the hallway's sheer curtains
I saw outlines of their dark silhouettes
and him reaching to hit her.
Something in me bubbled
and frothed like water on gas heat
a thermometer risen
an acceleration of years
pulp of my mother's bruises
fury that I'd experienced
being thrown against glass windows
shock as they broke over my shoulders
and feeling the kick of a slipper
as I lay in a crumpled heap.

Years later,
in Tompkins square Park
a fat redneck cop
tries to remove my friend
Michael and I from a public park
He asks for ID
and I laugh
hoping it echoes and
gurgles like blood
through the city streets
He grabs his nightstick
says "I'll give you something

to laugh about"
and I remember that rage coming
whenever I see a silver badge.

Seeing Kim
the tenor of my voice raises
I yell stop
Coward I say
and he hits me
the skin on my breasts tears
and Kim's voice goes papery
like a bird crying
Stop she says
you'll kill her.

The cops come
and I walk away
afraid to report him.
Weeks later Kim is seen
prostituting in Boston's combat zone.

It was a sad winter she left
I imagined her in a big white rabbit fur
standing on the glistening concrete
of Boston's combat zone.

# Eyes on the Prize

Shrouded in this circle of flames
is Emmett Till's face
bloated, beaten,
burning in my mind
every time I climb the stairs
to my house
sit in my kitchen
talk on my phone
I hear you asking me
why am I so angry
when I see little white ladies
in little white dresses
baking bread in brick ovens
while little white children play hopscotch
inside white picket fences

And I see
Emmett Till's body floating on a river
mutilated so badly
his mother could not say
who he was
bars split through him
for whistling at a white woman
his swollen face protruding
from that horrible picture
he was 14 years old
Do you hear me?

And I see white families celebrating,
no proof
no proof that 14 years old and Black
means any white man can kill you
for sport.

•

And I hear white laughter gurgling
from courtrooms
when they say you're free
to kill niggers wherever you like
Do you hear me?

You are free.

# Incest

My father wants to fuck me
and I want to fuck him
maybe it's the only way I know
to get love
the only way men know
to express emotion.

They say every father
wants to fuck his girl
it's the only way
they can control us.

I am so angry
I could kill
so angry
I'm afraid
angry
I fucked myself 30 years Daddy
I'm still protecting you
when truth is too hard
to face.

# Jealousy

Nothing prepared me
for the way she smiled at you . . .

In a totally unfeministic fantasy
I want to rip her apart
piece
      by
         piece
be a diva drag queen like Alexis Carrington
and tell her
"you have totally overstepped
your bounds"
as I withdraw my claws
recover my face
and pretend
you are a woman I loved
a long time ago.

# Precious Crazy Girl Giggles

Collard greens, bluefish, brown rice,
Junior's strawberry cheesecake
you are the sweet taste, main ingredient
season, summer, salt, cook, culinary artist
shake bake swing shuffle and shoo bee doo waaaa . . .

Midnight talks on the telephone
Frangelico, my favorite after dinner drink
Ethel Waters's skirt lifting
a serious shake bake swing shuffle
and shoo bee doo waaaa . . .

You are magic mommie
conjuring up ancestral spirits
when you swing your head back
and sing
releasing unrestrained laughter
please precious crazy girl giggles
feast for poor eyes
shake shake spin
and kiss
the morning we met.

# Why Did You Have to Be a Poet?

My mouth jammed
full of peanut butter
I'm stuck
contemplating my conviction
to kill you
penetrate your armor of aloofness
casual composure
poised disregard of the fact
my heart does handsprings
somersaults and splits
for your attention
sparks my inspiration
to imagine us in my bedroom
on a beach
emerald waters and white sand
squeezed through the fingers
you strip off my clothes
at sundown
I masturbate to a memory
of your face
the last time we argued
and I don't care
about your philosophies
your personal political persuasions
my question is
WHY DID YOU HAVE TO BE A POET?

Couldn't you be a doctor, nurse,
technician, anything
not to interfere in my career
of professional numbness
unaware and immune
to the music of your orchestra

a symphony of sound
strummed on broken guitar strings,
an echo of words overturned
sweetness swallowed, spit
and whispered in my ear
like a record scratched and spinning
I repeat
each song you quote
like scriptures
poetry is the only gospel
I know
there's no dictionary definition
for a person in love
with the rhythm of every word
you speak
and I crave you
like a cup of coffee
and a cigarette in the morning.

I haven't told you
how I talk to trees
about how my hands have grown huge
extending upward like branches
dark silhouettes against the sky
and how I hope they hold.

You slipped between my fingers
like liquid
a prisoner finding her way through
the opening at ends of a tunnel
and how my hands wandered lost
like sheep
a woman with no place to put
her psalms

And even this story is old
so old the roots have gone gray
even this story has stood
the twist and torment of teller
even the preacher knew
it wasn't Jesus
but loss
piled like logs
for a long winter

And somebody took the sound
someone took the sound
our mothers made
and the world built an arc
of our tears.

## Blues Suite

Black
bitter
coffee
morning
Blue night
steam on windows
your breath
I'm still trying to scrape off
still trying
to get this blue dye
out of my head
but that record keeps
scratching and moaning
moaning and scratching
your name.

Orange flames shooting up
over buildings
Blue firing squads
Black fumes
a cloud of ashes rising
from city to city
bomb blasts from country
to country
we interrupt this regularly scheduled programming
to bring you a special report
Black fumes
excuse me
fuming blacks
one thousand, no
ten thousand
fuming blacks
were seen marching down Main Street
PLEASE DON'T PANIC.

# Elegy

A gun shoved to my head
in a doorway dragged
skin clawing
insides splattering
blood drenched
gutter wails
I was midnight walking fast
stepping behind battle lines
drawn across Avenue C & D
East River shadows line up
my nostril
fists flared
beating against my face.

I knew Nelson before they did
crack and Colt .45
his dreads swinging laughter back
black spiraling up into and
out of his mind poems came
we all knew the dealer death squad
who chopped down his door
slammed a machete
through his foot
I knew him I did
I said I did
didn't I?

Early morning calls sleep
from someone twisting
a black bottle stem
scratching a rug
for remainders of a rock
searching for a speck of dust
flying from the roof of a tenement.

# Rapunzel

Rapunzel was a sister.
Think I'm playing?
I said, Rapunzel was a Black Woman.
That white woman with blond hair
hanging out in a castle
pining for Prince Charming
was a damn fairy tale!

Now, the Rapunzel I knew
had dreadlocks
longer than the Geechee River
I'd say "Rapunzel, Rapunzel!"
She'd say "What do you want now?"
I'd say "Rapunzel let down your hair"
and she'd let them dreadlocks
blond from baking in the sun
fall reluctantly from beneath
her red black and green cap
so I could grab hold of one and
climb on up.

We all know that fairy tale girl's hair
was too slippery to hold anyone
and anyway Prince Charming
should have left well enough alone
'cause I found out
the woman they said was a witch
keeping 'Punzel prisoner
was Rapunzel's lover
and that castle was the love
they built.

Yeah, Rapunzel was a free woman
making her own choices
and she did not need any rescuing.

# Underestimation of Power

When daddy pushed me and girlhood innocence
out my bedroom window
I picked up the shattered pieces of myself
and became a woman
HE UNDERESTIMATED MY POWER

I ran for my life
to a man I loved
and offered my dreams
to crouch in the shadows of his virility
until he left me
standing in a discotheque
pulsating rhythm penetrated my numbness
flashing neon lights restored my sight
I became his other lover's lover
HE UNDERESTIMATED MY POWER

When this woman said
I was sooo beautiful
so fine
my legs so long
she could slide
into the gulf of my heart
then rolled over
turned off the light
without ever reading my poems
SHE UNDERESTIMATED MY POWER

I lived in poems
wept in poems
hid in poems
and when a thief walked off
with three journals full

of my poems
I thought they'd walked off with me
I swore I'd never write again
I UNDERESTIMATED MY POWER

And when the principal said
and my mother said
and the supervisor said
I would never amount to anything
I became an artist
and made myself
THEY UNDERESTIMATED MY POWER

# Teaching

You can tell an abused kid
by inability to concentrate
unending need for attention
anger masked as sarcasm
and a need to please

Clinicians call them: sociopaths,
schizophrenics

At 16, I wonder
what they might have called me

I know people who've never come back
poets I respect
who are crazy in clinical terms

I prescribe poetry
pretend to be normal
and am more normal
than the people in charge
ego-centric
out of touch

My parents are the reason I teach
reason I cry
when kids tell me stories
deep down I identify
no one taught me
how to integrate
many selves into one body
15 years of education
didn't show how
to hold my head up
•

If my lessons aren't learned
I hope they remember respect
rules I broke by hugging
an emphasis on laughter
and questions not answered
but asked.

# Stretch Marks and Cellulite

Mirror, Mirror, on the wall
can't my feet be smaller, hair straighter,
thicker, shorter, longer
butt tighter, firmer
nose wider, thinner
eyes browner, bluer, greener
tits smaller, higher, rounder, less droopy?
Is there some way
I can get rid of these marks
stretched across my breasts, my ass
can't my legs be like silk stockings
and why do we have to scar at all
Mirror, Mirror, answer me.

I asked my lover if I have cellulite,
my trainer at the gym
a complete stranger and
a one night stand
Do I have it?

I want to be the object
of my own desire
lean and mean
like a sex machine
a brick house
solid as a rock
I want years of good nutrition
and to stop standing on my feet
forty hours a week
I want to look like
I've never worked at all
and never had to worry about it.
•

I have turned off lights
undressed undercover
wrapped fingers around
the thickness of your waist
my tongue tasted every
creamy saltwater concoction
your body could create
kissed between your toes
sides of your stomach
still I fear
the circus freak
500-hundred-pound lady
who commits suicide
to screams of laughter
we are buried in diets
anorexia
sunken sallow
skeletons of women
hidden in closets
for centuries
fat wraps
loofah
skin care products
*Vogue* and *Elle*
buy, sell yourself
squeezed in size 9 dresses
bones protruding from empty hips
and death is as easy as a *Cosmopolitan* diet
of grapefruit juice
vomit
vomit
every day more vomit
more blood we shit out
trying to be what we can't
keep dying
on operating tables from

liposuction
fat reduction
babies are born
and mothers don't always
regain their shapes.

# New York

They came from suburbs
Black, Latino, Asian, Indian
rich, middle, working class, white
from tops of their class
abundant refrigerators
well-balanced meals
they came
with fat cheeks and
plump behinds
to find no glamour, no lights, no fame.

With no guarantee they came
to high rents, no home at all
eviction notices, unemployment
jobs that paid under
5 dollars an hour
they came
to find brains and beauty
sold for less than the plane fare
they paid to get here.

They came to be discovered
not on the cover of *Deep Throat*
in back bars wearing baby dolls
g-strings, nothing at all
they came
afraid to leave
walking the streets
wanting someone, somewhere
to see, to help
and came to find desperation
in the fact no one would protect them

and some of them die here
but they're still coming.

*When we broke up*
*the radio only played ballads*
*by Joan Armatrading*
*and I sank into the earth*
*like ashes*
*unable to speak*
*night drew Black circles*
*around my eyes*
*and I stayed there a long time*
*examining each aspect of dust*
*as if they could answer*
*why.*

# Planet of the Apes

On Saturday afternoons
when chores were done
my mother and I would watch
Creature Double Feature on channel 56
My favorite: *Planet of the Apes*
with a scantily clad Charlton Heston
screaming "You dirty baboon
you killed my brother!"

Recently, someone told me
*Apes* was about Black people
I was aghast
Hollywood's response to civil rights
was a '70s sci fi about monkeys
who somehow did
but never in real life would
manage to survive a nuclear holocaust

One MOVE member did
manage to crawl from cinders of a police bomb
used in Vietnam special tactics
to tame 6 guerrilla fighters and 5 children
who wore dreadlocks

In Howard Beach,
the driver who hit and killed Michael Griffith
mistook a terrified Black man
for an orangutan crossing Queens Boulevard,
and was set free

27-year-old Michael Stewart
was murdered by police
as he aggressively painted a subway wall
•

11 Black boys who rape a white woman
in Central Park
are called a wilding wolfpack

Police shot and killed Eleanor Bumpurs,
a snarling, crippled 66-year-old Black woman
ankles and wrists tied together
stun-gunned
syphilis shot
labeled five-eighths human
the Tuskegee laboratory tests
fury rises as I remember Tarzan,
Charlton Heston as the Blond Blue Jesus
in Africa leading castes of monkeys
in a never ending series of rape,
battle, return to, conquest and escape from
planet of the apes

# It Is Not a New Age

When a gay man is beaten to death
in Harlem
disowned by family and friends
the government refuses to fund health care
and millions die from an epidemic
when disease is blamed on deviance
and bad blood
2 decades after Stonewall and civil rights
if I can't hold my lover's hand
on 125th Street
It Is Not a New Age

When a woman is dismembered
thrown 36 stories
abortion clinics bombed
social programs expendable
when Black people can't walk
in Bensonhurst, Boston or Haiti
It Is Not a New Age

6 years of college
fighting for rights
to speak my own language
if anger were an ax
it would split me open
and if this is a sermon
let it be my granddaddy's sermon
my grandmother's foottapping
steady rocking
choir singing
let it be Soweto
South Bronx
Tiananmen Square
cut back

set back
old-age
insecurity

I am further now
than I've ever been
reaching back to a religion
given up for an education
lacking color
lacking sound
broken, disjointed
fractured pieces of history
I keep searching for something
truer to me than crystals, harmonic convergence
Fellowship, my granddaddy would say
FELLOWSHIP
a community that cared
where people weren't hungry or
homeless
say it's not a new age
say it's not a new age
It Is Not a New Age

Part Two

# The Woods

Too far to turn back
too soon to go forward
so I'm stuck here
afraid

No one wanted to escape with me
everyone was too busy pretending
looked at me like I'd gone crazy
or possessed some secret strength
But, I just couldn't go on
with the same old things

All my life I've been owned
by someone, something
addiction
modern psych calls it "co-dependency"
always looking outside yourself
for answers

Well, I didn't want to belong to anyone
so I embarked
wanting to walk in the footsteps
of my favorites
Audre Lorde
Assata Shakur
Harriet Tubman

But, recovery has no road map
it's dark
I sleep in the woods
depend on the kindness of strangers
.

Do you know how long
I've walked in these shoes
how long since I've touched moss
on the north side of trees
my feet are worn
and weary from walking
and nowhere I go
is far enough
from where I was.

History hasn't told the truth about revolutionaries
you get some stupid image
of someone with superhuman strength
who doesn't hurt or experience everyday emotions
like Abbie Hoffman who committed suicide
after mobilizing the masses
Billie Holiday
one of America's greatest jazz singers
who drugged and drank herself to death
How many times did Harriet Tubman
wake up and say
I can't stand myself

I'm not bragging
about being a revolutionary
truth is
I left against my will
the earth started speaking to me
and everything bottled up
came out
parts of my flesh fell away
everything around me dark
my face unfamiliar

The first book anyone gave me
was a book about Harriet Tubman
how she helped rescue hundreds
what I don't know
is what she felt

# Monologue to God

Every time I gain some ground
you decide it's time to teach
me a lesson
I think my lessons should be limited
to once a week
I thought we agreed if I was good
I'd get a quick recovery
perhaps, I haven't suffered enough
Is there something I might do
to make you look upon my application
with more favor?
You're a man aren't you?

If I don't get a response
in five minutes
I'll drink, drug, fuck five women
There are ways
to get what I want
You aren't the only one with answers
who might possibly heal me
and I question if you're a figment
of some white man's imagination
created to keep us in shackles
and we're too busy searching for salvation
to question your credentials

Are you out of rainbows?
Decided not to send a signal
or save my soul?
What did Harriet see in you?

My grandparents worshipped you
24 hours / 7 days a week
and they both died poor, Black

horrible cancerous deaths
and when my grandmother got sick
I begged you over and over
don't let her die
and you let her suffer two years
until she finally withered away
It was Christmas
I don't even think she knew
who I was

I stopped believing in Santa Claus
even though I've always liked the basic idea
someone strong, protective, wise
like I wanted my father to be
you think I'd realize how
some things are never true
no matter how much I need
them to be

This is the end
of an extremely unfulfilling relationship
why don't you drop
into the deep blue sea
or better yet
find another job
something simple like
scrubbing my floor
doing my dishes
dropping dead
Does that sound like something
that might interest you?

And sincerely,
I hope no other girl believes in you
like I did
there's no point
in having her suffer.

Dear God,

I am dying
the seasons have stopped
and I can't move my legs

I give myself approximately
one hour and 15 minutes
to heal myself
during this time
I shall become a whole person.

Hello?!
Can you refer me to a therapist
someone Black, aware, educated
on all the issues
isn't afraid of lesbianism
doesn't know everyone I do?
Thanks.

Hello?!
75 dollars a session?
Tuesday at 12?
The address is?
Thanks!

Hello?
Someone less expensive
I'm OK.
Just sad right now.
Thanks.

Hello?!
I think I'm having a nervous breakdown

*did lots of drugs*
*left my lover*
*Why am I reacting this way?*
*Are you Black?*
*How do you feel about lesbianism?*
*Tuesday at 12.*
*Thanks.*

*The first therapist I went to*
*was a man*
*who kept asking why*
*was I a lesbian*
*when I told him*
*I was smoking crack*
*he said he'd give me drugs*
*that weren't dangerous*
*I actually don't have time*
*to be a slave*
*all of my friends*
*are doing shows . . .*

# The Artist

To liberate myself
I shall tell a story
the main character is me
and I'm in pain
if I bleed enough
I'll get a grant to travel
win the Pulitzer prize
be the first Black Woman
to capture the essence
of emotional enslavement
I shall transcend

How I feel is unimportant
writing is an intellectual exercise
full of semantics, structure and style

I should say something funny
so everyone will like me
and buy my books
It's indulgent to talk about myself
and talking about myself isn't art
Black lesbian writers are too angry
and our experience isn't universal
How much can I push down
trying not to offend anyone
adjust my emotions to a point
where they are socially acceptable
what's a poetic way to say
lonely
lost
enraged
•

I am not white, male, middle-class
and am supposed to know
how to hold myself
love myself above anyone else
I'm trying to say
when I was young
I was told to put a clothespin
on my nose
stay out of the sun
never be any different
than my neighbor next door
and am beginning to realize
it'll take more than a good book
two trainings on internalized racism,
sexism and homophobia
to get over it

I can't wait to show off my emancipation
surely writing will reflect how free I am

I haven't written since I started
searching inward
and won't get a Pulitzer prize
for simply surviving.

# The Revolutionary

Psychotherapy is indulgent,
self-pitying, bourgeois, a capitalist tool
to separate us from other people
our ancestors survived slavery, segregation
a 400-year holocaust
and they survived without psychotherapy.

Maybe we should take money we spend
pitying our plight as African Americans
and donate to the ANC.
Psychology has not articulated how racism,
sexism, homophobia and other
social, environmental issues affect us.
Until then,
it is symptomatic of a system
which enslaves us . . .

As a revolutionary
I don't just save myself
I save everyone
will go down in history
as someone who gave her life
to a greater cause.
I attend marches,
third world meetings,
organize against oppression everywhere
and am disappointed because
the revolution hasn't come
quick enough
entire organizations destroyed
by someone sleeping
with someone's lover
leaders who dominate

every discussion
women who abuse others . . .

Part of what propelled me
to become a revolutionary is
I believed everything was my fault
world wrong
because I was in it
and it was my obligation
to fix everything
run around trying to save everyone.
As a slave,
they say it's your fault.
There are so many slaves who valued
master's life over their own
he'd beat them
and the next day
slave came back
smiling harder than the day before
thinking if they tried
hard enough to please master
he wouldn't hurt them.
But, he did
and even though master couldn't see
how human slave was
slave could see
all of the circumstances
that made master cruel as he was.
So they forgave him again
and again.

Maybe that's why I'm so exhausted
as a revolutionary
I realize I can't save everyone
I'm trying to save myself
and I'm afraid

if I take one day off
I'll start saying:
The system works if you do.
I know the reason
my parents mistreated me
is their parents mistreated them
and slavery has destroyed
the psyche of every person in America
and they keep saying
we'll feel better
if we own a Volvo
and drink
and smoke
and eat
until we die
or just don't care at all
and I'm trying to stop myself
from forgetting the larger framework
from just not caring at all.
If the world tumbles tomorrow
it is not my fault
I've let enough people
kick and stomp me
into the 'ground
emotionally
and couldn't get angry
believing deep down
I deserved it
intentionally have put myself
in relationships I know will destroy me
because I can't get my mother
and father's voice out of my head
saying you deserve to die
and I still go home
to wish them a Merry Christmas

still smile
when I'm seething
still anguish
over other people's problems
still can't control anyone
except myself.

# Helpful Hints for an Aspiring Martyr

Find someone unable to assist themselves
avoid anyone independent or autonomous

overextend
immerse until indispensable
anger
independent thinking
are signs of ingratitude

Do anything to avoid conflict
if conflict is inevitable:
EXPLODE
call them selfish, self-centered,
unappreciative

Hold on to hurt
feelings of unappreciation forever
Build a wall of resentment around you

REPEAT PATTERN.

# Woman in Love 1

It's easy to be a slave
when you have someone.
We're both afraid to be alone
inept at intimacy
and have a tendency toward
self-destruction.

Something behind her eyes is explosive
and that makes her
the most exciting woman I've met.
She doesn't allow time
for writing and reflection
but, I don't care about myself.
I'm getting attention!
Even if I'm invaded,
her constant phone calls, cards
compliments are worth intrusion.

Most of my relationships have dissolved
and I'll do anything
to make this work
if only to prove to my last lover
and myself
I am capable of a lasting relationship.

Part of my attraction to her
is she actually believes I'm beautiful
and since I don't have eyes of my own
I rely on her to tell me
who I am.

I've stopped attending my meetings
the only person I still see on occasion

is my therapist.
I'm not healed
but love gives me time off
from soul searching.

# Woman in Love 2

She was my shelter.
I loved her
more than myself
and it feels like
someone has stripped off my clothes
and I'm standing in the street naked
with no place to go

She was not the most wonderful woman
I'd ever met
I broke up with her
I BROKE UP WITH HER
and wanted her to approve of me
breaking up with her
when we were together
I walked around asking everyone
Is this love
because I couldn't distinguish the difference
between love, obsession, dependency and abuse

I wanted someone to hold my hand
say I did a good job
Is that too much to ask for?
I've done everything, self-help
psychotherapy,
at night I even floss my teeth

This isn't the worst thing
I've ever lived through
I'll survive
like I survived summer camp
when that girl hit me
with a Dr. Scholl's shoe
•

But, all I want in this world
is my dignity
ability to wake up in the morning
and like what I see
Is that too much to ask for?

## Imagine Being More Afraid of Freedom than Slavery

The saddest thing in the world
has got to be
when you love someone
unable to provide the love
and support you need
and staying with them
would be a form of suicide.

It took all I had
to leave her
emotionally she still has a part of me
a year of therapy to resolve something
an honest conversation might have solved
and now I'm stuck
with everything I didn't say
and she's not here
to say it to.
I've tried to pretend it didn't hurt
as much as it did
searched all over this earth
for a safe place
and I can't walk up to somebody
and ask them
to give me back to myself
I just keep searching inside
hoping to find an answer
maybe she's my mother
maybe she's my father
maybe she embodies all the insecurity
I've ever felt and that's why
I keep coming back here
over and over I ask myself

Is it love?
But, it isn't desire
that drives me back to her
it's the fact
she has a piece of me I want
the pain to end
to belong to myself
and freedom to love someone
who loves me back.
I don't want any more illusions
no more women who appear powerful
and underneath have the emotional life
of a two-year-old
I'm keeping the same standard for myself
I am aware
and responsible for my life
and it's hard to believe that
want to give my power to anyone
anything passing by
because I'm terrified
to own myself.
If we owned ourselves
we'd overturn this earth
there would be no reason
to destroy everything we are
but it's easier and safer
to stay small.

In Nicaragua, one man
owned an entire peninsula
and all the food peasants picked
belonged to him
which they had to
after aching and sore muscles
buy back.
When the Sandinistas revolted

some of the peasants were given
their own land and machinery
but seven years later
the machines were still sitting there
unoperated
the people hadn't been taught
to take care of themselves
And in the 1800s
after that long war
some of the slaves
went back to the plantation.
Imagine being more afraid of freedom
than slavery
constantly sabotaging
and squeezing into places
too small for your potential
and even though you know this
you can't stop because
slavery is all you know.
They ask why?
Why don't women leave lovers
who abuse them
there is no land where we are free
I was not taught to honor myself
I'm painting a simple portrait
there are factors I haven't mentioned
like lovers who say
they'll kill us
declare us unfit for our children
no money
and no place to go.

In India, women are encouraged
to abort girl children
my mother was beaten so badly
the doctor said she'd die

and she stayed
But, I'm making a promise to myself
as this earth is my witness
I'm going to be free
I won't have to stand here
dragging these dead pieces of flesh
searching for a scrap of something
to cover myself
and maybe you never saw someone
fall to the floor
and ask God
for a way out of the wilderness
loved somebody so bad
you stumbled out like a rag doll
dragged across the coals.

When Harriet met John Tubman
he was the most beautiful man
something about his hands, his feet,
a back unscarred by slavery
and she dreamt
they'd settle somewhere
his arm across her shoulder
their lives firmly entwined
but slavery infiltrated
every aspect of their lives
sometimes it disguised itself
and other times it stood
an obstruction to every effort
and Harriet tried to explain
how earth was an invitation
how if she never saw the river
touched the trees
the sun would dry out of her eyes
and she would die
But, John saw himself

like a bird without wings
Aren't I enough, he'd ask,
and even though she left him
in the dry dust of a summer day
she felt abandoned.

The night Harriet left slavery
the wind spoke a strange song
an idiom without bass or baritone
the shrill sound of glass
a cry as she crept up to each cabin
and sang a spiritual
she looked over the landscape
and remembered how God spoke to Moses
through the burning bush,
Tell Pharaoh . . .

On Christmas, an old and dutiful slave
is waiting for Harriet's visit
but her daughter has gone North
that night the blues gave birth
to a paraplegic
a woman with no legs
the sound of cymbals
an earthquake
all over the world, wars
people plagued
by the same ills as their oppressor
The real revolution
is changing myself.

Harriet envisioned white women
extending their arms
thought freedom was a luscious land
something dramatic like in the movie *Roots*
when Alex Haley crosses the river

and upon seeing his ancestors says
*I found you*
*I finally found you*
or when Rocky defeats Apollo Creed
she must have been unprepared
to accept freedom as a process
a precious thing
that needs to be nurtured
being willing to start from scratch
leave a warm womb
for a world of winter, summer, fall
to live in unknown
and ultimately go where I want.

# Epilogue: Runaway

If you have the opportunity of traveling to Ghana and tour
Cape Coast Castle
built by the Portuguese to store sugar spices tobacco
Then used to warehouse Black slaves
You'll be shown male and female dungeons underneath
Dark black rooms, a window high above
Where food was tossed into the pit below
Pus larvae and feces
Slaves stood together crowded knee deep
There's a room to the side where rebels and
Troublemakers were kept separate so as
Not to incite the others
The order means slavery was not random
But an organized system
Sick and demented in nature
In Europe it was called the African service
where white men signed up went abroad
To not only capture slaves but for the promise of free
unlimited sex apart
From their wives
Most drank themselves to death or died of pox
There's even a chaplains room where the trade is presided
over
By religion and a Bible
These memories are vivid
I always imagine myself as the rebel
One kept separate, the runaway
Who received an even greater torture
Human muzzles built with iron and steel
Tongues cut out
Fingers hands feet amputated sawed off
Lacerations that looked like trees and maps
And roots
I've never questioned I was anything but a rebel and I've
paid dearly

Note to self:
The greatest punishments came from other slaves not the master
One of my poet sage friends says in response to my story
I know it's possible to be dragged for a long time
I am also a teacher whose led my students through art to fight the system
I didn't know though through all of this I was also the slave who surrendered my freedom
Couldn't imagine it for myself
Some part of me was held hostage
Ashamed to say I gave up
When the glorious day came and gold light shone over everything
The flowers and the crocus and every green living thing pushed itself
out of the ground to announce a new day
Birds took to the branches and sang Morning til night
The bold black letters of the news swung off the page
I stayed behind
Imagining as some did I was too old
Too scarred to go
Instead I enabled others . . .
So you can't imagine my surprise
When I discovered after a lifetime of labor
The fear that held me captive for so long
Began to dissipate
Knees bent
Toes grip ground
No more paralysis
I am running now


(2023)

Printed in the USA
CPSIA information can be obtained
at www.ICGtesting.com
JSHW021918280723
45588JS00002B/49

9 781531 504847